BOOK 5

SRa®

MULTIPLE SKILLS
SERIES: Reading

Third Edition

Richard A. Boning

Mc Graw Hill **SRA McGraw-Hill**

Columbus, Ohio

*A Division of The **McGraw·Hill** Companies*

Cover, Steve Bly/Tony Stone Images

SRA/McGraw-Hill

A Division of The **McGraw·Hill** *Companies*

Send all inquiries to:
SRA/McGraw-Hill
8787 Orion Place
Columbus, OH 43240-4027

ISBN 0-02-688438-0

5 6 7 8 9 BSE 06 05

PURPOSE

The *Multiple Skills Series* is a nonconsumable reading program designed to develop a cluster of key reading skills and to integrate these skills with each other and with the other language arts. *Multiple Skills* is also diagnostic, making it possible for you to identify specific types of reading skills that might be causing difficulty for individual students.

FOR WHOM

The twelve levels of the *Multiple Skills Series* are geared to students who comprehend on the pre-first- through ninth-grade reading levels.

- The Picture Level is for children who have not acquired a basic sight vocabulary.
- The Preparatory 1 Level is for children who have developed a limited basic sight vocabulary.
- The Preparatory 2 Level is for children who have a basic sight vocabulary but are not yet reading on the first-grade level.
- Books A through I are appropriate for students who can read on grade levels one through nine respectively. Because of their high interest level, the books may also be used effectively with students functioning at these levels of competence in other grades.

The **Multiple Skills Series Placement Tests** will help you determine the appropriate level for each student.

PLACEMENT TESTS

The Elementary Placement Test (for grades Pre-1 through 3) and the Midway Placement Tests (for grades 4–9) will help you place each student properly. The tests consist of representative units selected from the series. The test books contain two forms, X and Y. One form may be used for placement and the second as a posttest to measure progress. The tests are easy to administer and score. Blackline Masters are provided for worksheets and student performance profiles.

THE BOOKS

This third edition of the *Multiple Skills Series* maintains the quality and focus that have distinguished this program for over 25 years. The series includes four books at each level, Picture Level through Level I. Each book in the Picture Level through Level B contains 25 units. Each book in Level C through Level I contains 50 units. The units within each book increase in difficulty. The books within a level also increase in difficulty— Level A, Book 2 is slightly more difficult than Level A, Book 1, and so on. This gradual increase in difficulty permits students to advance from one book to the next and from one level to the next without frustration.

Each book contains an **About This Book** page, which explains the skills to the students and shows them how to approach reading the selections and questions. In the lowest levels, you should read About This Book to the children.

The questions that follow each unit are designed to develop specific reading skills. In the lowest levels, you should read the questions to the children. In Level H, the question pattern in each unit is

1. Title (main idea)
2. Stated detail
3. Stated detail
4. Inference or conclusion
5. Vocabulary

The **Language Activity Pages** (LAP) in each level consist of four parts: Exercising Your Skill, Expanding Your Skill, Exploring Language, and Expressing Yourself. These pages lead the students beyond the book through a broadening spiral of writing, speaking, and other individual and group language activities that apply, extend, and integrate the skills being developed. You may use all, some, or none of the activities in any LAP; however, some LAP activities depend on preceding ones. In the lowest levels, you should read the LAPs to the children.

In Levels C-I, each set of Language Activity Pages focuses on a particular skill developed through the book. Emphasis progresses from the most concrete to the most abstract:

First LAP	Details
Second LAP	Vocabulary
Third LAP	Main ideas
Last LAP	Inferences and conclusions

SESSIONS

The *Multiple Skills Series* is basically an individualized reading program that may be used with small groups or an entire class. Short sessions are the most effective. Use a short session every day or every other day, completing a few units in each session. Time allocated to the Language Activity Pages depends on the abilities of the individual students.

SCORING

Students should record their answers on the reproducible worksheets. The worksheets make scoring easier and provide uniform records of the children's work. Using worksheets also avoids consuming the books.

Because it is important for the students to know how they are progressing, you should score the units as soon as they've been completed. Then you can discuss the questions and activities with the students and encourage them to justify their responses. Many of the LAPs are open-ended and do not lend themselves to an objective score; for this reason, there are no answer keys for these pages.

A careful reader thinks about the writer's words and pays attention to what the story or article is mainly about. A careful reader also "reads between the lines" because a writer does not tell the reader everything. A careful reader tries to figure out the meaning of new words too. As you read the stories and articles in this book, you will practice all of these reading skills.

First you will read a story and choose a good title for it. The title will tell something about the **main idea** of the article or story. To choose a good title, you must know what the story or article is mainly about.

The next two questions will ask you about facts that are stated in the story or article. To answer these questions, read carefully. Pay attention to the **details.**

The fourth question will ask you to figure out **something the writer doesn't tell you directly.** For example, you might read that Dr. Fujihara received an emergency call, drove to Elm Street, and rushed into a house. Even though the writer doesn't tell you directly, you can figure out that Dr. Fujihara knows how to drive and that someone in the house is probably sick. You use the information the author provides plus your own knowledge and experience to figure out what is probably true.

The last question will ask you to tell the meaning of a word in the story or article. You can figure out what the word means by studying its **context**—the other words and sentences in the story. Read the following sentences.

Clara ran out to the garden excitedly. Vegetables were growing in neat rows in the small, raised beds. Each bed was surrounded by flowers. Clara was not interested in the vegetables. She wanted to see the daisies and the bright yellow *marigolds.*

Did you figure out that marigolds are flowers? What clues in the story helped you figure this out?

This book will help you practice your reading skills. As you learn to use all of these skills together, you will become a better reader.

Sonja Henie was perhaps the most popular and well-known ice skater in the world. She also was certainly one of the top moneymakers.

At the age of ten, Sonja won the Norwegian national championship in figure skating and was an overnight sensation in her homeland. She won the Norwegian skating title five more times and the all-European title for eight consecutive years. Between 1927 and 1936, Sonja won ten world ice-skating championships and was awarded three gold medals at the Olympic Games of 1928, 1932, and 1936.

Sonja Henie first came to the United States for an ice-skating tour of the country. She starred in the first ice show, the Hollywood Ice Revue, which was a huge success. Moving permanently to the United States, Sonja made ten movies before her *demise* in 1969. She was one of the greatest skaters of all time.

---

1. The best title is—
   (A) Sonja Henie Wins the Olympic Games
   (B) Sonja Henie—A Famous Skater
   (C) Hollywood Ice Revue—The First Ice Show
   (D) Traveling Around the United States

2. The story says that Sonja appeared in—
   (A) five Olympic Games　　　　(B) many magazines
   (C) Moscow　　　　　　　　　 (D) ten movies

3. Sonja Henie first came to the United States—
   (A) by accident　　　　　　　(B) for a skating tour
   (C) to help poor children　　 (D) to be in movies

4. The story suggests that Sonja first learned to skate in—
   (A) the United States　　　　(B) Iceland
   (C) Norway　　　　　　　　　(D) Canada

5. The word "demise" in line twelve means—
   (A) popularity　　　　　　　(B) success
   (C) birth　　　　　　　　　　(D) death

It is *primarily* a time when the ice starts to melt, the trout season opens, smoke rises from the sugarhouses, and, yes, the roads are muddy. But it's also a time for a most unusual celebration. Haven't you heard? It's "Mud Time!" New Englanders will proudly point out to you that the poet Robert Frost celebrated this special season in his poem "Two Tramps in Mud Time."

In Montpelier, Vermont, this brief period between winter and spring is a special time for celebration. What does one do at Mud Time? You can buy Mud Season greeting cards, of course. You can watch wood-carvers demonstrate their skills or watch the cows join in the annual Mud Time Parade. If you're more athletic, you can go snow skiing, canoeing, and mountain biking. More than forty-thousand visitors attend the Annual Vermont Maple Festival. Maple syrup is the prime local product during this period. What a sweet season it is!

---

1. The best title is—
   (A) Sweet Maple Syrup
   (B) Robert Frost's Poem
   (C) Muddy Roads
   (D) The Joys of Mud Time

2. The story says that Mud Time occurs—
   (A) in the springtime
   (B) in the wintertime
   (C) between winter and spring
   (D) when the roads turn icy

3. The main product sold at the annual festival in Vermont is—
   (A) maple syrup
   (B) greeting cards
   (C) poems
   (D) mud

4. The story suggests that Mud Time—
   (A) is a boring time
   (B) is a fun time
   (C) occurs all over the country
   (D) occurs without notice

5. The word "primarily" in line one means—
   (A) in the second place
   (B) seldom
   (C) chiefly
   (D) sometimes

After forty years, Antonia Brico finally received the fame she deserved. She became known the world over as a great orchestral conductor.

Antonia was born in Holland in 1902 and was educated at the University of California. In those days, most orchestras in America were not interested in women conductors, so she went to Europe. When she was twenty-eight, she became the first woman to conduct the Berlin Philharmonic Orchestra. In 1930, Antonia returned to America to lead the Los Angeles Philharmonic and was a great success. She then went back to Europe to conduct that continent's greatest orchestras.

Antonia came back to America in 1974 to once again lead the Los Angeles Philharmonic Orchestra. It was a *stirring* performance that firmly established her as a great conductor. She was seventy-two years old at the time.

1. The best title is—
   (A) Traveling Through Europe
   (B) The Los Angeles Philharmonic Orchestra
   (C) A Famous Woman Conductor
   (D) An American Education

2. Antonia Brico was born in—
   (A) Berlin   (B) Holland
   (C) Los Angeles   (D) Italy

3. Antonia Brico first conducted in—
   (A) California   (B) Holland
   (C) America   (D) Europe

4. The story suggests that Antonia Brico was—
   (A) never successful in   (B) devoted to music most of her
       the United States   life
   (C) a great pianist   (D) not very talented

5. The word "stirring" in line eleven means—
   (A) silent   (B) poor
   (C) exciting   (D) forgotten

Raphael ranks among the *foremost* artists of all time. His paintings hang in many of the world's greatest museums. Yet it is said that he once traded away what has since become a masterpiece for a bit of food!

One evening the great painter saw a mother singing to her small child. As is often the case with artists, he was inspired to paint the scene—but there was no canvas to paint on! Raphael spied an old barrel nearby and used its round cover as his canvas. The story is that he sold the painting to a tavernkeeper for a meal worth less than fifty cents, though he was not a poor man.

The Italian government sent the painting to the New York World's Fair in 1939, where it was exhibited. It now hangs in a palace in Florence, Italy—and is valued at over $1,000,000!

---

1. The best title is—
   (A) A Poor Painter
   (B) The 1939 New York World's Fair
   (C) The Story of a Raphael Painting
   (D) Raphael and Other Artists

2. The painting in the story was painted on a—
   (A) canvas   (B) barrel cover
   (C) scrap of paper   (D) piece of cloth

3. Raphael sold the painting to—
   (A) the Italian government   (B) the World's Fair
   (C) a tavernkeeper   (D) a palace in Florence

4. The story suggests that great paintings can become—
   (A) less valuable as time goes by   (B) lost easily
   (C) more valuable as time goes by   (D) faded

5. The word "foremost" in line one means—
   (A) least known   (B) most important
   (C) youngest   (D) worst

Take a good look at your houseplants. If you knew what they could do, you'd never take them for granted again. For example, did you know that some common houseplants, such as philodendrons, are poisonous if you eat them? Keep your cats away from them!

Plants may not exactly be smart, but they're not helpless. The wild potato will *emit* a chemical when its leaves are attacked by insects known as aphids. The chemical, in effect, acts to warn the aphids of danger, and the aphids try to escape. Marigold leaves also contain a chemical that bugs dislike. Releasing chemicals is a way many common plants have of fighting back against the insects and animals that want to eat them. Where do the plants get their chemicals? They manufacture these substances themselves.

Plants are not just pretty things to look at or good defenders. People benefit from them. Some of our most important medicines come from plants.

---

1. The best title is—
   (A) Potatoes and Marigolds
   (B) Watch Out for Aphids!
   (C) Plant Power
   (D) Pet Cats, Beware!

2. Many plants fight off insects and animals by making—
   (A) leaves   (B) aphids
   (C) chemicals   (D) wild potatoes

3. The story says that philodendrons are—
   (A) pretty   (B) poisonous
   (C) leafy   (D) manufactured

4. Houseplants will release chemicals when they need to—
   (A) grow leaves   (B) make their own food
   (C) take medicine   (D) protect themselves

5. The word "emit" in line six means—
   (A) detect   (B) release
   (C) escape   (D) attack

There's a strange animal running around that resembles a knight in a suit of armor. Early settlers in Louisiana and other parts of the South discovered this creature and called it the *armadillo*, meaning "little armored one."

The armadillo is like a walking tank. It has bony shields over its upper body. Underneath, however, the unprotected body parts are *vulnerable*. The body shield is made up of bands or plates of bone connected by flexible skin. Shields also cover the legs and the top of the head. Nature did not forget the animal's tail. It, too, is usually encased in bony rings.

What does an armadillo do when it faces an enemy? For one thing, it doesn't have to attack. The armadillo just rolls itself into a ball or simply presses its unprotected belly against the ground. Instantly the animal is like a fortress. There is no question that the shields are quite effective, but because of them the armadillo may be the strangest-looking animal in America.

---

1. The best title is—
   (A) A Knight's Suit of Armor
   (B) Animal Tanks and Shields
   (C) The Strange-looking Armadillo
   (D) Body Shields

2. Bony shields cover the armadillo's—
   (A) belly   (B) body except for the head
   (C) entire upper body   (D) body except for the tail

3. In the story, the armadillo is *not* compared to—
   (A) a knight   (B) a tank
   (C) a fortress   (D) a turtle

4. The armadillos' shields are nature's way of—
   (A) decorating the animal   (B) tricking humans
   (C) attacking other animals   (D) protecting the animal

5. The word "vulnerable" in line five means—
   (A) protected   (B) able to be harmed
   (C) dangerous   (D) able to destroy

"I'll not do it," said the doctor as he stalked out of the room. "I'll not perform surgery with a woman assistant." Five other men followed him, and Doctor Bethenia Owens-Adair was left alone. It was 1872, and women were not welcome in the medical profession.

Bethenia Owens-Adair had always been a rebel. Just a few years earlier, she had left her native Oregon and enrolled in medical school, where she earned her doctor's degree. Three years after her son had become a doctor, she earned another degree in medicine.

As a surgeon, Doctor Owens-Adair performed many *surgical* procedures before she retired in 1905 and gained great fame for these operations. But she always remembered the time, many years earlier, when other doctors had refused to work with her.

---

1. The best title is—
   (A) A Medical School in Oregon
   (B) The First Operation
   (C) Doctor Owens-Adair
   (D) Doctors in the 1800s

2. The story says that Bethenia had always been—
   (A) kind to animals   (B) athletic
   (C) a traveler   (D) a rebel

3. In the late 1800s women were not welcome in—
   (A) churches   (B) the medical profession
   (C) beauty contests   (D) restaurants

4. The story suggests that Dr. Owens-Adair became a doctor despite—
   (A) a lack of education   (B) a lack of money
   (C) an illness   (D) prejudice

5. The word "surgical" in line nine means—
   (A) difficult   (B) referring to school
   (C) referring to an operation (D) unnecessary

Children often surprise their parents by bringing home strays to adopt as pets. Nan Lincoln of Maine shocked her children by bringing home a seal pup that had been *abandoned* by its mother.

Lincoln first saw the pup hiding behind a rock. After long and careful observation to be sure that the seal's mother was not returning, Lincoln took the furry creature home. She fed the weak pup from a bottle to help it gain strength. The seal, whom she named Cecily, gradually gained weight, happily watched television, and went for short swims with its new family.

Although the family had grown to love Cecily, they knew that their pet would return to the sea someday. They sent the pup for longer swims until, when they were sure she could survive, they painted a bright yellow stripe on Cecily's back and let their friend swim off to join a colony of seal pups. The Lincolns miss Cecily, but they know the sea is the best home for a seal pup.

1. The best title is—
   (A) A Seal Watches Television
   (B) A Seal Pup Is Saved
   (C) Families Adopt Many Strays
   (D) A Bright Yellow Stripe

2. Lincoln fed the pup from a bottle to make it—
   (A) warm   (B) friendly
   (C) tired   (D) strong

3. Cecily left the family to live with—
   (A) ocean scientists   (B) a seal colony
   (C) another family   (D) other strays

4. The story suggests that the yellow stripe made Cecily—
   (A) hard to find   (B) very uncomfortable
   (C) funny to look at   (D) easy to spot

5. The word "abandoned" in line three means—
   (A) comforted   (B) born
   (C) left alone   (D) badly hurt

Are your table manners medieval? During the Middle Ages—or medieval period of history—Europeans *consumed* food using their fingers. It was considered good manners to use three fingers of the hand to eat with, but not all five. People rarely used forks or spoons. When did forks become acceptable? Not really until the eighteenth century! Spoons were accepted somewhat earlier as practical implements—especially for eating liquids such as soups.

The only eating utensil found at a medieval table was the knife. When guests were invited to dinner at someone's house, usually they were expected to bring their own knives. They would use knives both to spear hunks of meat to put on their plates and to cut their meat. Knives were also used to cut the plates. This made sense because these "plates" were made of heavy bread! Guests were expected to share drinking cups and bowls of food.

How did people keep their hands clean during a meal? First they wiped their fingers on pieces of bread and then wiped their hands on the tablecloth. What a mess!

---

1. The best title is—
   (A) Spoons and Forks Were Forgotten
   (B) Modern Rules for Eating at the Table
   (C) Medieval Table Manners
   (D) Messy Foods in the Middle Ages

2. The only eating utensil used in medieval times was the—
   (A) spear   (B) spoon
   (C) fork   (D) knife

3. The story says that plates were made of—
   (A) china   (B) meat
   (C) clay   (D) bread

4. Manners during the Middle Ages were—
   (A) not as refined   (B) very delicate
       as today's
   (C) more refined than today's   (D) the same as today's

5. The word "consumed" in line two means—
   (A) cooked   (B) licked
   (C) ate   (D) prepared

It is 10:29 A.M., and Raymond Abreu, who *resides* with his family in an apartment in the Bronx, in New York City, is balancing eggs on end. The eggs are actually standing on their own on this special day. It may not seem so unusual unless you have tried it. If you ever have tried this stunt, you know that the egg will almost always fall. Many people believe that it is possible to stand an egg on end only once a year and only at a special moment in time—the moment of the vernal equinox.

What is the vernal equinox? It is the time of year when night and day are of equal length—twelve hours each—everywhere in the world. At this time, the sun is directly above the equator. This usually occurs about March 21 and marks the beginning of spring in the Northern Hemisphere.

Why might you be able to balance an egg on end at this time only? No one really knows for sure, but people like Raymond Abreu, who have tried it, look forward to this "egg-citing" annual event!

1. The best title is—
   (A) March 21 or Thereabouts
   (B) Fun in the Bronx
   (C) An In-depth Study of the Equator
   (D) A Special Moment for Egg Balancers

2. The vernal equinox marks the beginning of—
   (A) autumn   (B) winter
   (C) spring   (D) the egg-hunt season

3. During the vernal equinox, night and day are—
   (A) longer than 24 hours   (B) both 21 hours long
   (C) shorter than 24 hours   (D) each 12 hours long

4. The story suggests that Raymond Abreu balanced the eggs because—
   (A) he was lucky   (B) he is a stunt man
   (C) it was a warm day   (D) it was during the vernal equinox

5. The word "resides" in line one means—
   (A) travels   (B) lives
   (C) claims   (D) stands

Gertrude Palmer was honored by Californians in 1989 as the state's Senior Adult Student of the Year. She told the crowd of well-wishers: "Try to learn something new every day. It keeps you young." Palmer should know, for at the age of 105, she was still learning and still feeling young.

Oddly enough, she had just completed a course called Effective Living for Seniors. Palmer's forty-nine-year-old instructor said about her: "Gertrude's so rich in life experience that she teaches me more than I teach her."

What event in history stood out most for this woman, who was born in 1883 in England? It was a *milestone* that took place in the nineteenth century. She remembered Queen Victoria's 1897 Diamond Jubilee, the celebration of the monarch's sixtieth anniversary as Queen. Her memory of the parade of troops and blaring bands had stayed as fresh as last week's news.

---

1. The best title is—
   (A) School Days
   (B) The Diamond Jubilee
   (C) Still Learning at 105
   (D) California Student

2. Gertrude Palmer received an award for—
   (A) Teacher of the Year   (B) Senior Adult Student of the Year
   (C) Californian of the Year   (D) Effective Living for Seniors

3. The advice Palmer gave was—
   (A) to keep active   (B) to learn something new
   (C) to keep young   (D) to go to England

4. You can tell that Gertrude Palmer was—
   (A) athletic   (B) competitive
   (C) poor   (D) enthusiastic

5. The word "milestone" in line nine means—
   (A) defeat   (B) an important event
   (C) march   (D) large rock

In 1882, one of the most spectacular and talked-about attempted train robberies in history took place in Nevada. A train was going across the country to the East, carrying a valuable cargo. A man named Ross, who was assigned as a guard, knew that he had to be on the lookout for holdups. People always seemed to know when something valuable was being moved by railroad.

Suddenly, armed bandits rode up on horseback and ordered the train to stop. The engineer obeyed. They told Ross to get out, but he refused and stayed inside with the door locked. The robbers shot at the car. They even forced the engineer to smash another car into the car holding Ross and the money. Still Ross remained inside. After three hours, the sheriff and his men arrived. The would-be train robbers, who were still trying to break into the car, were arrested. Through it all, Ross had not budged from inside the car, *obstinately* refusing to give up. He became known as "Hold-the-Fort Ross."

---

1. The best title is—
   (A) The Tale of Hold-the-Fort Ross
   (B) Bandits on Horseback
   (C) A Valuable Cargo
   (D) A Famous Robber

2. The attempted train-robbery took place in—
   (A) Montana   (B) Nevada
   (C) Colorado   (D) Wyoming

3. When the sheriff and his men arrived, the robbers—
   (A) escaped   (B) laughed
   (C) killed them   (D) were arrested

4. The story suggests that Ross—
   (A) was foolish   (B) was killed
   (C) was dedicated   (D) received a reward

5. The word "obstinately" in line twelve means—
   (A) stubbornly   (B) sadly
   (C) weakly   (D) doubtfully

In Unit 1, you read about the triumphs of the Norwegian ice skater Sonja Henie. Now read about an American athlete who became a champion on ice 40 years later.

Eight-year-old Peggy Fleming sat on the changing bench at the edge of the rink and laced up her first pair of ice skates. Her older sister Janice recalls with amazement how Peggy stepped onto the ice and glided away from the changing bench without so much as a wobble. Peggy was a natural from the start. That day marked the beginning of her career. By 1965, she had already won three United States figure-skating championships and was busy preparing for the world figure-skating competition. She practiced five hours a day, six days a week. The effort was grueling, but her hard work paid off. When the judging was over, she had become the first American woman to win a world figure-skating championship since 1960. In 1968, she was the only American to win an Olympic gold medal.

Peggy Fleming became known for her special style of skating. She performed with a natural grace and ease. Since her retirement from amateur skating, Peggy Fleming has worked to promote the cause of women's sports in the United States.

A. Exercising Your Skill

The passage above tells you that Peggy Fleming achieved great success as a skater. Some of the information also lets you know *why*. Find at least three sentences or phrases that contain this kind of information. Discuss with your classmates what each sentence or phrase shows about Peggy Fleming and how the quality that it shows is related to her success.

B. Expanding Your Skill

Finding out the history of a sport can be very interesting. For example, if the English game of "rounders" hadn't been changed into a game called "town ball" in the United States, then baseball might never have been invented. Choose one of the following sports or another one that you prefer. Then, using an encyclopedia or any other source of information, find out how that sport got started. Take notes as you read.

bobsledding	gymnastics	speed skating
football	soccer	tennis
basketball	bowling	golf

Organize your notes into chart or outline form to answer questions such as these: *When and where did the sport originate? Who contributed most to its beginnings? Why did it become popular? How was it played at first?* Then report your findings in class.

C. Exploring Language

What sport do you like to play or watch the most? Write a three-paragraph report about your favorite sport. In the first paragraph, describe briefly the basic object of that sport. In the second paragraph, tell about what equipment is needed, if any, and how much practice time is required. In the third paragraph, explain how you became interested in the sport and why you still enjoy it. Write your reasons in a way that might convince others to try the sport. Illustrate your report with pictures cut from magazines or newspapers, your own drawings, or personal snapshots. Write captions for your illustrations.

Gather your and your classmates' reports. Organize the reports by subject. Then make a class book entitled "Our Favorite Sports" for all to read and enjoy in their free time.

D. Expressing Yourself

Choose one of these activities.

1. Write a letter asking for information about figure skating. For example, you might ask what kind of skates are the best to use or where in your area skating lessons are given. Send your letter to:

   United States Figure Skating Association
   20 First Street
   Colorado Springs, Colorado 80906

2. Go to the library and find information about another famous woman figure skater, such as Carol Heiss or Dorothy Hamill. Then compare information about that skater with what you read about Sonja Henie in Unit 1. Your comparison may be organized in chart form or paragraph form.

3. Take a survey of your friends, relatives, and neighbors. Ask everyone these questions: *What sport do you enjoy playing the most?* and *What sport do you enjoy watching the most?*

   When you have finished, make a "fact sheet" that includes all your results. What were the most popular and least popular sports mentioned? What sport(s) did people most enjoy both playing *and* watching? Get together with other classmates and compare your results. Work together to make up a display summarizing these results.

4. Most people would agree that exercise is important for a person's physical health. Others would go a step further. They would say that exercise is also important for a person's *mental* health. What reasons or facts can you think of that support this opinion? What reasons or facts might actually make the opinion seem not valid? Have a class debate that argues the second issue.

From the beginning, Mary McLeod Bethune's parents knew that she was destined to do something special. Born in South Carolina in 1875, the fifteenth child of former slaves, Mary was the first of the children to be born free.

Education was to serve Mary well throughout her life. In 1895 she began a teaching career. Then, in 1904, she opened a girls' school in Daytona Beach, Florida. The school was *merged* in 1923 with a boys' school and together they formed a new college, Bethune-Cookman College.

Mary McLeod Bethune was an advisor on eduction to several U. S. Presidents—Coolidge, Hoover, and Franklin Roosevelt. When Eleanor Roosevelt invited her to tea at the White House, Bethune was well aware that she was often the first woman to hold distinguished positions, as well as the only black person to receive the many honors awarded her for her public service.

Mary once wrote in her diary: "I know so well why I must be here, must go to tea at the White House. To remind them always that we belong here, we are a part of this America."

---

1. The best title is—
   (A) An Invitation to Tea
   (B) Educated Black Americans
   (C) Destined to Do Something Special
   (D) Mary McLeod Bethune's Diary

2. Mary McLeod Bethune's school became a college in—
   (A) 1875   (B) 1904
   (C) 1895   (D) 1923

3. The story says that Bethune became a presidential—
   (A) teacher   (B) advisor
   (C) speech writer   (D) tea hostess

4. You can tell that Bethune was honored and respected as—
   (A) a writer   (B) a White House visitor
   (C) an educator   (D) a White House reporter

5. The word "merged" in line six means—
   (A) assembled   (B) built
   (C) changed   (D) joined

Arch Deal was a Florida television newscaster who had made over seven hundred parachute jumps. He was scheduled to jump as one of the special events celebrating the annual Festival Month at Cypress Gardens, Florida. However, something went wrong in the jump, and Deal's chute *malfunctioned*. He plummeted to earth, crashing into an orange grove. Rescuers first thought Deal was dead, but despite a broken neck, back, and leg, as well as internal injuries, he pulled through—and vowed to jump again.

On the first anniversary of his accident, at the same time of day, using the same plane, same pilot, and same chute, Deal again stepped into space over Cypress Gardens and began to tumble earthward. He counted and pulled the parachute cord. For two heart-stopping seconds, nothing happened. Finally Deal felt the lifesaving jolt of the chute's opening. Crowds below sighed in relief. Arch Deal had gambled that history would not repeat itself—and he had won.

1. The best title is—
   (A) Festival Month at Cypress Gardens
   (B) Arch Deal—A Famous Television Newscaster
   (C) How Parachutes Save Lives
   (D) Arch Deal Tries Again

2. When Arch Deal had his accident, he—
   (A) broke his back   (B) didn't get hurt
   (C) quit parachuting   (D) landed in water

3. On the first anniversary of his accident, Deal—
   (A) was still in the hospital   (B) was still unable to walk
   (C) jumped again   (D) was seriously injured

4. You can tell from the story that Deal had extraordinary—
   (A) talent   (B) courage
   (C) vision   (D) parachutes

5. The word "malfunctioned" in line four means—
   (A) looked beautiful   (B) was found
   (C) worked well   (D) didn't work

Many of the facts of Molly Pitcher's life are not known for sure, but we do know enough to place her high on the list of heroic women of the American Revolution.

At the beginning of the Revolution, Mary McCauley's husband *enlisted* in the army as a gunner. Mary herself soon left her Carlisle, Pennsylvania, home to join him in camp. At the Battle of Monmouth, on June 28, 1778, she earned the nickname that would go down through history—Molly Pitcher—by carrying pitchers of water to the exhausted and thirsty troops. When her husband was wounded, she took over his cannon and helped to win the important battle. In 1822, the state of Pennsylvania granted her a pension for life. A state monument was raised in her honor in 1916, and on the Monmouth, New Jersey, battle site a bronze plaque shows Molly, her cannon, and a water pail.

Molly was honored again in 1928 with a special U.S. stamp.

---

1. The best title is—
   (A) A Special U.S. Stamp
   (B) The Death of Molly Pitcher
   (C) A Brave Woman of the Revolution
   (D) Famous Battles of the Revolution

2. Molly Pitcher was granted a pension in—
   (A) 1822   (B) 1778
   (C) 1916   (D) 1928

3. The story says that Molly's husband was a—
   (A) blacksmith   (B) British soldier
   (C) stamp collector   (D) gunner

4. The story suggests that Molly Pitcher—
   (A) had many children   (B) made cannons
   (C) lived many years after the battle (D) was killed during the battle

5. The word "enlisted" in line four means—
   (A) rebeled   (B) signed up for duty
   (C) was captured   (D) deserted his post

At what age should a football coach be required to retire? If you had asked Amos Alonzo Stagg, the question would have gone unanswered for a long, long time.

Stagg, who was born in 1862, coached football for forty-one years at the University of Chicago. At the age of seventy, he was forced to retire. However, retirement at that age proved to be *premature* for Stagg. He moved to the College of the Pacific and worked there as head coach for the next fourteen years. Again, college officials asked him to retire because of his age. You can probably guess that the now elderly Stagg took another job. This time he went to Stockton Junior College, where he became the kicking coach. Finally, in 1960, he retired. By then, Stagg was ninety-eight years old! He died at the "young" age of 102. Don't you agree that Amos Alonzo Stagg deserves the title of "the grand old man of football"?

---

1. The best title is—
   (A) A Football Coach
   (B) Retirement Age for Coaches
   (C) How to Coach Football
   (D) A Coach Too Young to Retire

2. Stagg was first forced to retire at the age of—
   (A) 41   (B) 70
   (C) 98   (D) 102

3. Stagg's last coaching job was at—
   (A) Stockton Junior College   (B) the high school level
   (C) the College of the Pacific (D) the University of Chicago

4. The story suggests that Amos Alonzo Stagg—
   (A) was not a good coach   (B) liked to change jobs
   (C) liked to work   (D) didn't like to coach

5. The word "premature" in line six means—
   (A) unexpected   (B) on time
   (C) too late   (D) too soon

Members of fire departments and police departments often visit children's classrooms. They tell the children about their work and what the children should do in case of emergency. The officer who visited the classroom of Hilary Canaran, in Doylestown, Pennsylvania, saved her house from being destroyed!

Hilary was in kindergarten when an officer from the fire department spoke to her class. She remembered how *informative* the officer had been, telling what to do if a house catches on fire. A year later, when Hilary was six years old, a fire started in her kitchen. She immediately called the operator and asked for the fire department. The fire department took her address and told her to leave the house. Hilary picked up her three-year-old sister and her cat, then went outside to wait for the fire trucks.

Hilary's house was saved and the fire chief praised her prompt action.

---

1. The best title is—
   (A) The Fire Department of Doylestown
   (B) A Lesson in School Saves a House
   (C) How to Prevent Fires
   (D) Police Officers Visit Schools

2. Hilary learned what to do in case of fire when she was in—
   (A) kindergarten   (B) first grade
   (C) second grade   (D) high school

3. The fire in Hilary's house started in the—
   (A) cellar   (B) attic
   (C) living room   (D) kitchen

4. The story suggests that young Hilary was—
   (A) not careful   (B) slow to act
   (C) quick thinking   (D) quite friendly

5. The word "informative" in line seven means—
   (A) incorrect   (B) unhappy
   (C) giving details   (D) giving money

How do you know if a train is going eighteen miles per hour? The president of the Transit Authority (TA), who *oversees* the vast network of subway trains and buses in New York, wants to know! The operators of the subway trains in that city do not really know.

The problem is that the city subway system does not use speedometers. These speed indicators are used on everything from exercise bikes to jumbo jets. Operators in nearly every major subway system in North America have speedometers. They are standard equipment in Boston, San Francisco, and Cleveland—but not in New York City. Why not? "They would be too difficult to maintain," said one TA spokesman.

Eighteen miles an hour is the safe speed at which the trains should travel in certain zones. For now, the New York subway operators have nothing to rely on but their experience. Watch out for speeders!

---

1. The best title is—
   (A) Speedometers
   (B) A Subway System Without Speedometers
   (C) Major Subway Systems in North America
   (D) Riding the Subway

2. Speedometers are *not* used on subway trains in—
   (A) North America
   (B) Boston
   (C) New York City
   (D) Cleveland

3. When it comes to knowing how fast they are traveling, New York subway operators depend on—
   (A) passengers
   (B) their brakes
   (C) speedometers
   (D) their experience

4. The story suggests that subways without speedometers are—
   (A) more common
   (B) slower
   (C) more modern
   (D) more dangerous

5. The word "oversees" in line two means—
   (A) crosses the sea
   (B) rides in
   (C) supervises
   (D) fails to notice

The crowd watched, open-mouthed, hundreds of feet below. The thought must surely have crossed their minds: "What if the straps should break?" Well, they didn't, and Sandi Pierce provided a thrilling spectacle as she went through her aerial act.

The airplane, piloted by Sandi's husband, Walt Pierce, looped, rolled, twisted, and turned through the sky at speeds over 160 miles per hour. Sandi rode the wing. She walked the wing. She even danced gracefully on the wing. Walt, a pilot since he was 15 years old, also taught Sandi to fly, and at times the two of them performed daring stunts, each in a different plane. The high point of the Pierces' act occurred when Walt flew the plane upside down, and Sandi dangled, head down, waving to those below.

Sandi, not content to stay with the plane, also made parachute jumps. Would you say Sandi was *amazingly* adventurous?

---

1. The best title is—
   (A) The Sport of Parachute Jumping
   (B) The Dangers of Flying
   (C) A Woman Does Daring Stunts in the Air
   (D) Walt Pierce—A Pilot at Fifteen

2. The high point of Sandi's act occurred when she—
   (A) danced on the wing   (B) hung upside down
   (C) fell into a lake   (D) flew the plane alone

3. One of Sandi Pierce's stunts was—
   (A) crashing a plane   (B) flying through fire
   (C) walking on the wing   (D) jumping without a parachute

4. The story suggests that Sandi Pierce is not—
   (A) afraid of heights   (B) happy
   (C) afraid of the dark   (D) married

5. The word "amazingly" in line thirteen means—
   (A) slightly   (B) unfairly
   (C) never   (D) unbelievably

England's Grand National Steeplechase—a long course with thirty jumps—is the most difficult horse race in the world. Few horses finish the race; sometimes none do. In 1904, the great Australian champion, Moifaa, won the race, but the champion horse's victory in getting to England was far more spectacular.

The ship carrying Moifaa from Australia sank during a terrible storm. The passengers and crew crowded into the lifeboats. Everyone forgot about the horse, locked in its stall. Suddenly, a huge wave smashed against the ship and opened the stall door. Moifaa was washed overboard into the violent seas. The *valiant* horse bravely battled the waves. Finally, it reached an island fifty miles from the place where the ship had sunk. There were no other survivors.

Near death, Moifaa was found by some fisherman who lived on the island. They shipped the horse back to England, where it recovered and won the famous race.

1. The best title is—
   (A) England's Grand National Steeplechase
   (B) The Dangers of Ocean Travel
   (C) A Sea Journey to Australia
   (D) An Incredible Horse Named Moifaa

2. According to the story, the Grand National Steeplechase is—
   (A) fun to watch   (B) the most difficult race
   (C) the easiest race   (D) not popular today

3. The story says that the Grand National Steeplechase has—
   (A) low jumps   (B) six jumps
   (C) high jumps   (D) thirty jumps

4. The story suggests that when the boat sank, the people—
   (A) were angry   (B) were thinking clearly
   (C) radioed for help   (D) panicked

5. The word "valiant" in line ten means—
   (A) fearful   (B) courageous
   (C) angry   (D) violent

When the family car breaks down, the power fails, or the water main bursts, we begin to realize what life was like before modern conveniences. Ann Marie Sikorski went back to that life. Born in Clearwater, Florida, Ann Marie bought a 100-acre farm in the mountains at Berea, Kentucky. She had no television and no running water! She tended sheep, pigs, and other farm animals, *cultivated* her own tomatoes, pumpkins, and green vegetables, and did her own weaving and quilting.

Ann Marie grew to appreciate the old ways of living when she started camping in the Georgia mountains during her college years and later, as a social worker, when she helped aged farm people. She was surprised to see that so many of these men and women, with little money and no cars, electricity, or running water, were quite satisfied. It was then that she decided to live like them. What many people would consider a hard life became a happy life for Ann Marie.

1. The best title is—
   (A) Modern Conveniences Make Life Easy
   (B) The Mountains of Georgia
   (C) A Woman Who Likes the Old Ways
   (D) Farmers and Their Problems

2. Ann Marie Sikorski bought a farm in—
   (A) Georgia   (B) Florida
   (C) Colorado   (D) Kentucky

3. Ann Marie found the aged farm people—
   (A) unhappy   (B) quite wealthy
   (C) well educated   (D) satisfied

4. The story suggests that Ann Marie was—
   (A) weak   (B) rugged
   (C) unhappy   (D) humorous

5. The word "cultivated" in line five means—
   (A) bought   (B) grew
   (C) disliked   (D) removed

Where is the largest privately owned ranch in the United States? It is on the Big Island of Hawaii—225,000 acres of ranch land at the foot of the snowy peaks of Mauna Kea. This is where the Parker Ranch was founded in 1847 by John Palmer Parker.

In the early 1800s, most Northerners who wanted to be ranchers or cowhands headed toward Texas and other western states. In 1809, Parker, a sailor from Massachusetts, ended up in Hawaii instead. He started out with a small plot of land given to him by King Kamahameha, who united the Hawaiian Islands. In 1816, Parker married one of the king's granddaughters. Their combined properties were the beginning of the *extensive* Parker Ranch lands.

Many of the hundred ranch hands there today are descendants of the original Parker Ranch "paniolos," or cowhands. They tend the fifty-thousand head of cattle and four-hundred horses. For the first time in its 142-year history, paying guests are now allowed to visit the ranch.

---

1. The best title is—
   - (A) The Parker Ranch "Paniolos"
   - (B) Sailing to Ranch Land
   - (C) The Biggest Ranch on the Big Island
   - (D) A Gift to a Sailor

2. The Parker Ranch is located in—
   - (A) Texas
   - (B) Massachusetts
   - (C) the North
   - (D) Hawaii

3. Parker's first plot of land was given to him by—
   - (A) a sailor
   - (B) a king
   - (C) a cowhand
   - (D) his granddaughter

4. The story does *not* tell—
   - (A) how Parker learned the ranching business
   - (B) where the ranch is located
   - (C) the size of the ranch
   - (D) when the ranch was founded

5. The word "extensive" in line ten means—
   - (A) outdoors
   - (B) broad in action
   - (C) unbroken
   - (D) large in area

The inscription on the Sullivan Memorial Trophy awarded to Wilma Rudolph reads: "To the athlete, male or female, who by performance, example, and good influence did the most to advance the cause of good sportsmanship."

What are the chances that a young black child, unable to walk, will grow up to be an award-winning athlete? Wilma Rudolph defied doctors who said that one of her legs was useless after she had a bout with double pneumonia and scarlet fever. After many difficult treatments and exhausting work, six-year-old Wilma could walk with the help of specially made shoes. As a teenager, she was a good basketball player, but she *excelled* at running—to the extent that she was good enough to participate in the 1956 Olympic Games in Melbourne, Australia.

Rudolph's time of glory came in the 1960 Olympics. She became the first American woman to win three gold medals in track and field in the same Olympic Games. Rudolph was soon called "the gazelle" in Europe. In America she was still known by the nickname of Skeeter—a darting, buzzing mosquito.

---

1. The best title is—
   (A) Wilma Rudolph's Best Years
   (B) Wilma Rudolph's Triumphs
   (C) Olympic Stars
   (D) Still Known as Skeeter

2. As a young child, Wilma Rudolph—
   (A) was in the Olympics
   (B) ran faster than her friends
   (C) could not walk
   (D) was called the "gazelle"

3. At the 1960 Olympics, Rudolph—
   (A) won the Sullivan Memorial Trophy
   (B) won for being a good sport
   (C) played basketball
   (D) won three gold medals

4. Americans called Rudolph "Skeeter" because she—
   (A) looked like a mosquito
   (B) was also a skater
   (C) was so fast
   (D) was annoying

5. The word "excelled" in line nine means—
   (A) was superior
   (B) preferred
   (C) failed
   (D) was popular

The scarecrow—a crude figure of a person dressed in old clothes—is a familiar sight on a farm. Because crows like to eat grain, they are considered a nuisance to farmers. Therefore, farmers set up scarecrows in the fields to scare crows and other birds away from the crops.

Scarecrows frighten birds because the figures look like human beings, right? Don't believe it! It is neither the look on the scarecrow's face nor the old clothes that scare the birds. In fact, smell has everything to do with the scarecrow's *effectiveness*. It seems that the scent of a person on the scarecrow's clothes is actually what frightens the birds off.

The scent factor works only for a time, however. When rain and wind have done their job, the clothing on the scarecrow loses its human smell. Then the scarecrow is nothing more than a colorful, decorative display in the field.

---

1. The best title is—
   (A) The Secret of a Scarecrow's Success
   (B) Crows—A Nuisance to Farmers
   (C) Scarecrows Are Scared
   (D) Human Scent

2. Scarecrows are supposed to frighten—
   (A) farmers   (B) crops
   (C) snakes   (D) birds

3. What really frightens the birds away is the scarecrow's—
   (A) clothing   (B) crude shape
   (C) face   (D) human scent

4. The story suggests that when the scarecrow's clothing loses its human scent the scarecrow—
   (A) is most frightening   (B) is thrown away
   (C) doesn't scare the birds (D) makes the crops smell

5. The word "effectiveness" in line eight means—
   (A) development   (B) production of desired result
   (C) popularity   (D) enthusiasm in the field

In Unit 20, you read the words *sometimes, lifeboats,* and *overboard.* These words were formed by joining two words together. Many words have been created either this way or in other, even more interesting, ways. Read this passage.

The English language is constantly changing. New words are being added, and some words are being dropped from lack of use. How words come into English is often very interesting. Many words, of course, are simply "borrowed" from other languages. For example, from Native American languages English has borrowed words such as *opossum* and *skunk.*

Words have also come into English in unusual ways. For example, many of our words, such as *cupcake, daydream,* and *goldfish,* are compound words that were formed by joining two short words. Other words are formed in a similar way. Instead of two complete words being joined together, however, parts of two words are blended together. If, for instance, you blend the words *flash* and *glare,* you get *flare,* or if you blend *slop* and *slush,* you get *slosh.* Other words are simply shortened. *Bike,* for example, is the shortened form of *bicycle,* and in current everyday conversation, *max* or *maxi* is the shortened form of *maximum.* Still other words, such as *buzz* and *crunch,* are echoic—created to imitate sound. All of these ways of adding words make English a fascinating, lively language.

A. Exercising Your Skill

Number your paper 1–8. Read each numbered item below, and write the word that belongs in each blank. Then, in small groups, discuss which words are formed by (a) joining two words, (b) blending two words, (c) shortening a long word, or (d) imitating a sound.

1.   thorough + bred = _____
2.   the echoic word or words for the sound a horn makes = _____
3.   shortened form of *microphone* = _____
4.   motor + hotel = _____
5.   skate + board = _____
6.   shortened form of *telephone* = _____
7.   the echoic word for the sound a clock makes = _____
8.   splash + spatter = _____

B. Expanding Your Skill

As you discussed the words in Part A, did you think of other words that are formed in these unusual ways? Make four columns on a piece of paper. Write one of these words at the top of each column: Joining, Blending, Shortening, and Imitating. Then write as many words under each column as you can. Let the dictionary help you think of words.

C. Exploring Language

The following words have been formed by joining, blending, shortening, or imitating. On a piece of paper, first write how each word was formed. Then write one sentence for each word. Try to show the meaning of the words in your sentences. Let a dictionary help you.

1.	hiss	6.	glimmer
2.	brunch	7.	boom
3.	earthquake	8.	gym
4.	thunderstorm	9.	telecast
5.	champ	10.	lifetime

Compare your answers and sentences with those of your classmates. If some of the answers or uses of words in sentences vary, discuss the reasons for these variations. See if you get any new ideas or want to make any changes.

D. Expressing Yourself

Choose one of these activities.

1. In small groups, try to make up some brand new words! Use any, some, or all of these four methods: combining, blending, shortening, imitating. Take turns presenting your words to the rest of the class and having your classmates guess their meanings.

2. Words have come into the English language in ways other than those mentioned in Part A. Some words are actually the names of people or places. For example, when you ride a Ferris wheel, remember that the man who invented that ride was named George Ferris. When you eat a hamburger, remember that it was named after the city of Hamburg, Germany. Look in the dictionary and find the person or place the following words are named after.

> pasteurize   limerick   maverick   braille   cheddar

3. How could your first or last name—or the name of someone you know—become a word that everyone uses? Most often, people's names are used for something they invented or discovered. Think of something you would like to have named after you. Draw a picture of it and write a definition for it.

In the game of chess, queens and kings are important playing pieces. In the world of international chess competition, the Polgar sisters from Budapest, Hungary, were royalty themselves. Knowledge of the three sisters never became *universal,* but they made a mark in the history of the game.

The oldest sister was Szusza (Susan), who was ranked as the third-best female chess player in the world at age 19. Not to be outdone, 12-year-old Judit, the youngest Polgar sister, ranked number one. Zsofi (Sofia) scored a remarkable eight victories against grand masters, or top players, from Russia and the West.

For all three Polgar sisters, getting to the top had its price. They practiced six hours a day and traveled worldwide at least six months out of the year. How did the girls feel about working so hard? Susan's explanation was simple. "It's our job; it is what we do."

1. The best title is—
    (A)   Hungarian Children
    (B)   The Game of Chess
    (C)   Queens of the Chessboard
    (D)   Grand Masters in Competition

2. The Polgar sisters were from—
    (A)   Russia   (B)   the West
    (C)   Hungary   (D)   the South

3. The Polgar sister ranked number one in chess was—
    (A)   Susan   (B)   Judit
    (C)   Sofia   (D)   Zsofi

4. The story suggests that the Polgar sisters took their game—
    (A)   seriously   (B)   jokingly
    (C)   for granted   (D)   nervously

5. The word "universal" in line four means—
    (A)   challenged   (B)   unknown
    (C)   evident at home   (D)   present everywhere

A big dispute broke out in San Francisco, California, in the 1920s. The ferryboats that carried people north from the city across San Francisco Bay were overcrowded. Many people suggested a bridge. Some people called it "The Bridge That Couldn't Be Built."

Joseph B. Strauss, a world-famous bridge builder, said he thought it could be built. Finally, work was started. One construction worker said, "There was one earth *tremor* when I was up on top. The ground shook so hard, we didn't think the bridge would make it. We figured the whole thing would drop into the water."

It didn't drop. The bridge was erected and it has become the best known bridge in America—the Golden Gate Bridge.

---

1. The best title is—
   (A) The Stormy San Francisco Bay
   (B) A World-famous Bridge Builder
   (C) Building the Golden Gate Bridge
   (D) San Francisco in 1920

2. The Golden Gate Bridge is in—
   (A) California   (B) South Dakota
   (C) Connecticut   (D) Canada

3. The story says that one problem in building the bridge was—
   (A) lack of money   (B) calm waters
   (C) an earth tremor   (D) a tornado

4. The story suggests that the bridge was built because of—
   (A) people out of work   (B) too much money
   (C) overcrowded ferryboats (D) rough waters

5. The word "tremor" in line seven means a—
   (A) fireball   (B) trembling
   (C) hailstorm   (D) sunset

Long ago, when John Mullins discovered that he had a strange talent, his life began to change. People sought him out to find water. Did he use a fancy instrument, a map, or a special machine? No, Mullins simply used a forked stick. He did the actual digging himself. He asked only a modest fee and traveling expenses for each job he undertook.

Mullins would grip one part of the forked stick in each hand and hold the point of the stick straight up. Then he would walk over an area. If the stick dipped sharply down to the ground by itself, Mullins knew he had surely found water under the ground.

This technique for locating water underground goes back to the 1500s in Germany. John Mullins practiced his "art" in the 1800s in England. The technique still has its believers and nonbelievers today. It is not *foolproof*. Sometimes it works, and sometimes it doesn't. When it does work, no one can explain why.

1. The best title is—
   - (A) Underground Water Reserves
   - (B) Finding Water with a Stick
   - (C) Believers and Nonbelievers
   - (D) A Modern Art

2. John Mullins located water with a—
   - (A) fork
   - (B) straight stick
   - (C) map
   - (D) forked stick

3. Mullins knew he had located water when the stick—
   - (A) pointed upward
   - (B) broke in his hands
   - (C) dipped sharply down
   - (D) fell to the ground

4. The story suggests that locating water with a forked stick—
   - (A) works every time
   - (B) is a new technique
   - (C) is not necessarily scientific
   - (D) usually is the best technique

5. The word "foolproof" in line twelve means—
   - (A) always safe
   - (B) always reliable
   - (C) strong
   - (D) foolish

Can a building be so ugly that people get angry just looking at it? For years the Old Executive Office Building (the OEOB) in Washington, D.C., received more than its share of insults. President Warren G. Harding proclaimed that the building was "the worst I ever saw." Mark Twain described it as the "ugliest building in America."

At a cost of ten million dollars over seventeen years of construction, the OEOB was completed in 1888. For many, it was hate at first sight. The building was used for many purposes over the years and then fell into neglect.

Then one day in 1974, a college student named John W. F. Rogers was working in the mail room of the White House. He was sent to get a chair in one of the OEOB "storerooms." Rogers thought he had entered "the castle of the Sleeping Beauty." Everything was covered in dust and cobwebs, he recalls, "and yet I saw beauty." Years later, Rogers became the *administrator* of the building. Once he was in charge, one of the first things he did was to restore the old "storeroom." It is now the grand White House Law Library!

1. The best title is—
   (A) The Story of John W. F. Rogers
   (B) Sleeping Beauty
   (C) The Story of the Old Executive Office Building
   (D) A Change of Scenery in Washington, D.C.

2. The Old Executive Office Building is in—
   (A) a castle
   (B) New York City
   (C) Washington, D.C.
   (D) a storage area

3. One person who saw beauty in the OEOB was—
   (A) Mark Twain
   (B) Sleeping Beauty
   (C) President Harding
   (D) John W. F. Rogers

4. The story suggests that the OEOB fell into neglect because—
   (A) the White House needed storerooms
   (B) it cost too much to maintain
   (C) people found it so ugly
   (D) it was old and dusty

5. The word "administrator" in line thirteen means—
   (A) mail-room clerk
   (B) carpenter
   (C) architect
   (D) manager

For the first forty-two years of her life, Rosa Parks lived a quiet, normal life. Then on December 1, 1955, Rosa Parks took a fateful bus ride in Montgomery, Alabama. She was returning home from her job as a seamstress. When the bus driver ordered Parks to give up her seat to a white man, she refused. Rosa Parks was arrested and fined ten dollars for violating the city's law that kept black people and white people separated in public places.

This incident sparked the Civil Rights Movement. Black community leaders in Montgomery, under the leadership of Dr. Martin Luther King, Jr., took action. They boycotted, or refused to use, the city's buses. After 382 days, nationwide public support for the boycott forced the city to change its law. Thereafter, black people could sit wherever they wanted on city buses.

Rosa Parks became a symbol for the blacks' struggle for civil rights. For her *invaluable* role, she was known as the "mother of the Civil Rights Movement."

1. The best title is—
   (A) Riding a Bus
   (B) The Mother of the Civil Rights Movement
   (C) The History of Montgomery, Alabama
   (D) Dr. Martin Luther King's Leadership

2. Rosa Parks made history by refusing to—
   (A) ride a bus
   (B) return home after work
   (C) drive a bus
   (D) give up her seat on a bus

3. The incident in Montgomery happened in—
   (A) 1955
   (B) 1942
   (C) 1951
   (D) 1910

4. The story suggests that the public believed that Rosa Parks was—
   (A) Dr. King's mother
   (B) not helpful to blacks
   (C) not a good worker
   (D) not treated fairly

5. The word "invaluable" in line thirteen means—
   (A) not lucky
   (B) of great importance
   (C) of little value
   (D) very wealthy

In the early 1800s, oil was obtained mostly by hand, gathered from the tops of some streams and springs. This method seemed good enough at the time.

However, in 1859, the first successful oil well was drilled by Edwin L. Drake, at Titusville, Pennsylvania. Drake's idea that there was oil "beneath" the ground was an entirely new one. Many people laughed when he set up his odd–looking *rig*, but he scraped together a small amount of money and started drilling. On August 27, he struck oil and thus began one of the biggest industries in the world today.

When Drake's well ran dry, he sold the land around it for only $10,000. He invested the money in the stock market and lost everything. In 1873, the state of Pennsylvania provided Drake with a pension of $1,500 per year for life. He died in 1880, a famous man who had made little from a great discovery.

---

1. The best title is—
   (A) A Man Who Made a Million Dollars
   (B) Pennsylvania—A Wonderful State
   (C) Edwin Drake and the First Oil Well
   (D) A Growing Industry

2. Edwin L. Drake died in—
   (A) 1859   (B) 1873
   (C) 1880   (D) 1907

3. When Drake invested his money in the stock market, he—
   (A) lost everything   (B) became rich
   (C) was a child   (D) asked for a pension

4. The story suggests that Drake had—
   (A) many enemies   (B) a large family
   (C) no friends   (D) bad luck

5. The word "rig" in line six means—
   (A) school   (B) country
   (C) equipment   (D) stream

Albert Kanter loved good literature, but he couldn't get his own children to read it. They preferred comic books. In a desperate effort to interest his children and others, he began the Classic Comic Books Company in 1940. The first comic book he published was one of his own favorite stories, "The Three Musketeers," based on a novel by Alexandre Dumas. It was, to his surprise, a success.

Soon to follow were other classic stories such as "Tom Sawyer," "Romeo and Juliet," and "David Copperfield." Their success was probably due to three factors: the covers were bright and attractive, the stories exciting, and the writers kept the style of the original books but made them easier for children to read.

All the books ended with a short reminder expressing hope that the reader would be *motivated* enough to read the original book. The reader often was!

1. The best title is—
   (A) The History of Classic Comic Books
   (B) Studying Good Literature
   (C) "Tom Sawyer"—An Exciting Story
   (D) Why Children Want Comic Books

2. The story says that covers on Classic Comics were—
   (A) dull
   (B) humorous
   (C) attractive
   (D) made of cardboard

3. The first Classic Comic Book was—
   (A) "Tom Sawyer"
   (B) "The Three Musketeers"
   (C) "Romeo and Juliet"
   (D) "David Copperfield"

4. The story suggests that when the original stories were printed in Classic Comics—
   (A) children didn't like them
   (B) they were made longer
   (C) the style was changed
   (D) the stories were made simpler

5. The word "motivated" in line twelve means—
   (A) frightened
   (B) inspired
   (C) unhappy
   (D) young

UNIT 32

There was once a very spoiled little girl named Victoria. She refused to study and often had fits of temper. A governess was hired to help raise and educate Victoria, and she was no longer permitted to do everything that she wanted. When her governess told her that she had to learn more than other girls did, Victoria wanted to know why. Her governess, however, wouldn't tell her.

One day when Victoria was eleven, she had a great surprise. She picked up her history book to study, and in it she noticed a slip of paper on which were written the names of all the kings and queens of England. Much to her surprise, she saw her own name written at the bottom of the list, under that of her uncle, whom she called "Uncle King." She knew then that she would someday become queen of England. From that time *hence,* no one had to remind Victoria to study very hard.

1. The best title is—
   (A) Queen Victoria's Manners
   (B) Victoria's Important Discovery
   (C) The Governess of an English Queen
   (D) A Famous History Book

2. Victoria was told by her governess to—
   (A) learn more
   (B) study less
   (C) ask for anything
   (D) avoid reading

3. The story says that Victoria was once very—
   (A) sweet
   (B) athletic
   (C) ill
   (D) spoiled

4. Victoria apparently realized that studying was important for—
   (A) a governess
   (B) her uncle
   (C) a future leader
   (D) kings

5. The word "hence" in line eleven means—
   (A) forward
   (B) backward
   (C) today
   (D) yesterday

Cindy Scott had an important hobby. She was one of 11,000 volunteers across the United States who checked local weather for the National Weather Service. When the woman who had been recording the weather in her town retired, Cindy was glad to take her place. What made Cindy unusual was that when she began her weather watch, she was only nine years old.

Outside Cindy's home was a large electronic thermometer. Every evening, without fail, Cindy *diligently* checked it to record the day's high and low temperatures. A tape indside the thermometer box continuously recorded information. At the end of each month, Cindy removed the tape and sent the monthly totals to the weather station in Albuquerque. She measured rainfall and snowfall and recorded the information.

Cindy became the local weather expert. She received calls from gardeners, campers, and outdoor workers who relied on her information to make their plans.

---

1. The best title is—
   (A)   The National Weather Service
   (B)   Volunteer Workers
   (C)   Young Weather Watcher
   (D)   Life in New Mexico

2. Cindy Scott supplied information about—
   (A)   electronics   (B)   weather
   (C)   thermometers   (D)   gardening

3. Cindy sent weather information to Albuquerque—
   (A)   every night   (B)   once a year
   (C)   every month   (D)   once a week

4. The story suggests that weather watching—
   (A)   is only for adults   (B)   provides useful information
   (C)   is of little use   (D)   must be done by scientists

5. The word "diligently" in line seven means—
   (A)   earnestly   (B)   lazily
   (C)   foolishly   (D)   quickly

Fire has been both one of humanity's greatest friends and one of its most terrifying enemies. To the Hackler family of Indiana, fire became a most puzzling mystery.

The first fire broke out one morning in a room upstairs. Firefighters put it out with no difficulty, but before they reached their firehouse, the Hacklers had reported another fire. The blaze came from some papers between the mattress and springs of a bed. A total of nine separate fires broke out in the Hackler home that morning. A calendar, a pair of overalls, a book—all were burned up at different times. The Hacklers moved out of the house to the front yard. Local firefighters, mystified and *fatigued*, called for help from neighboring communities.

Eventually, the Hacklers tore down their home and built another. The insurance company called it "a complete mystery."

---

1. The best title is—
   (A) A House and Its Unexplained Fires
   (B) How Fires Help Humanity
   (C) The Importance of Fire Prevention
   (D) A Mysterious Insurance Company

2. The first fire started in—
   (A) the cellar   (B) an upstairs room
   (C) the front yard   (D) the garage

3. One thing burned in a fire was a—
   (A) beautiful rug   (B) lamp
   (C) book   (D) chair

4. Fire has been called "humanity's greatest friend" because it—
   (A) is a mystery   (B) can burn us
   (C) has red flames   (D) can keep us warm

5. The word "fatigued" in line ten means—
   (A) happy   (B) weary
   (C) rested   (D) strong

There are some people who go on to do extraordinary things despite the odds against them. Wildfire, or Edmonia Lewis, as she later called herself, was *decidedly* such a person.

Edmonia's mother was Chippewa, and her father was black. In 1859, she attended Oberlin College in Ohio. It was rare for *any* woman to attend college at that time in history, let alone a woman who was part African American and part Native American. Oberlin was the first U.S. college to accept women and blacks.

Edmonia Lewis used her heritage and her talent to build a career as a sculptor. Her Native American roots are evident in her work *Old Arrow Maker*. Her loyalty to her black roots is reflected in one of her first works, a medallion of the abolitionist John Brown, who was killed for his work in trying to free slaves.

Edmonia Lewis was a woman of strength and character. She became a respected artist in her time. Unfortunately, most of her sculptures were either lost or destroyed, but her reputation lives on.

---

1. The best title is—
   (A) A Woman at Oberlin College
   (B) Nineteenth-century American Sculpture
   (C) The Story of Edmonia "Wildfire" Lewis
   (D) A Native American's Heritage

2. Edmonia Lewis' formal education went as far as—
   (A) high school   (B) college
   (C) graduate school   (D) Oberlin Elementary School

3. Edmonia Lewis' loyalty to her roots is reflected in her—
   (A) sculpture   (B) diary
   (C) painting   (D) jewelry

4. The story suggests that Oberlin was a—
   (A) New England college   (B) prejudiced college
   (C) progressive college   (D) foreign college

5. The word "decidedly" in line three means—
   (A) uncertainly   (B) unhappily
   (C) by chance   (D) without a doubt

Problems, problems! Some would-be problem solvers are so overwhelmed by the problem that they usually fail. There are others who approach the problem calmly and practically, and usually solve it. Still others—only the truly *inventive*—find a unique solution to the problem in order to prove a point.

For example, Alexander the Great, an ancient Greek ruler, was said to have been challenged to untie the Gordian knot. In mythology, this knot was fastened to a wagon and was thought to be impossible to undo. The great ruler was able to accomplish the task easily, however. He simply cut the knot with his sword!

Tradition has it that Christopher Columbus was once given a challenge, too. In 1493, he attended a banquet in his honor, where he was questioned about how he had coped with the difficulties of his voyage to the New World. Columbus replied by challenging his questioners to balance an egg. When they couldn't, he did. How? He cracked the shell to create a flat bottom!

1. The best title is—
   (A) Two Wise Problem Solvers
   (B) Alexander Unties the Knot
   (C) Problem Solving Today
   (D) Columbus Had a Way with Eggs

2. Alexander the Great undid the Gordian knot—
   (A) with an egg   (B) with a wagon
   (C) with a sword   (D) by cracking it

3. Christopher Columbus balanced an egg—
   (A) by slicing it   (B) by tying it
   (C) by cracking it   (D) by sailing to the New World

4. The story suggests that some difficult problems are best—
   (A) solved by science   (B) solved by one person
   (C) forgotten   (D) solved the easy way

5. The word "inventive" in line four means—
   (A) good at making up fancy lies   (B) good at thinking up something new
   (C) not versatile   (D) not creative

The early airplanes had open cockpits and were unheated. It is no surprise, therefore, that a common complaint of the pilots who flew these planes was the coldness they suffered. Leave it to Harriet Quimby to find an effective solution for the cold weather!

There were few women pilots in the early days of flying. Harriet Quimby made a lasting impression in aviation history in more ways than one. Soon after taking flying lessons, she set new records. In 1911, Quimby was the first woman in the United States to receive a pilot's license. Then, in 1912, she became the first woman in the world to pilot a plane across the English Channel.

How did this pilot not get cold? Of course, she wore *cumbersome* layers of clothing, including a wool coat and a raincoat, on top of her satin flying suit. However, Quimby credited something other than clothing with helping her the most. When she landed the plane after her historic flight, Quimby felt fine—a hot water bottle had kept her warm!

1. The best title is—
    (A) The First Woman in an Airplane
    (B) Historic Pilot Wins Battle over Cold
    (C) Harriet Quimby Takes Flying Lessons
    (D) Crossing the English Channel

2. Early pilots complained of the cold because their planes—
    (A) flew across water   (B) were open and unheated
    (C) didn't have hot water   (D) were air-conditioned

3. Quimby made history crossing the English Channel because she—
    (A) was the first U.S. woman   (B) was an unlicensed pilot
        to do so
    (C) was the first woman in the (D) took flying lessons
        world to do so

4. When it came to keeping warm, Quimby was—
    (A) impatient   (B) brave
    (C) practical   (D) unconcerned

5. The word "cumbersome" in line ten means—
    (A) lightweight   (B) thin and graceful
    (C) wasteful   (D) heavy and awkward

"The mail must go through!" That's a slogan of the United States Postal Service. It means no matter what happens, important mail must be delivered. One man who believed that was John Thompson. He had been born in Norway but came to America as a boy. He lived in Placerville, California, near the Sierra Mountains.

In Thompson's day, more than 100 years ago, heavy snows often made it impossible for mail carriers on horseback to deliver letters across the mountains to Nevada. But Thompson had a good idea. He remembered how people traveled in deep snow in Norway—on skis, which were then called "snowshoes." So Thompson began *toting* people's mail over the Sierras on snowshoes/skis. He became famous and people called him "Snowshoe" Thompson.

Today, cross-country skiers have a race every winter in his honor, and a statue of "Snowshoe" Thompson stands tall and proud near the mountains.

1. The best title is—
   (A) The U.S. Postal Service
   (B) "Snowshoe" Thompson
   (C) The Snows of Norway
   (D) Snowshoe Races

2. John Thompson was born in—
   (A) California
   (B) Norway
   (C) Nevada
   (D) Colorado

3. Thompson lived—
   (A) less than 100 years ago
   (B) more than 200 years ago
   (C) more than 100 years ago
   (D) his whole life in Placerville

4. We can tell that the weather in Norway is—
   (A) always warm
   (B) sometimes cold
   (C) sometimes hot
   (D) never cold

5. The word "toting" in line ten means—
   (A) touching
   (B) mistaking
   (C) accepting
   (D) carrying

Can your pet do "tricks"? Are pets smarter than we think? Read this passage. As you read, look for the main idea of the passage.

Too quickly and too often, people label animals *dumb*. Well, those people haven't studied animal behavior. Sea otters, for example, live in the ocean and love to eat shellfish, but there's just one problem: how to crack open the shells. The clever sea otters solve that problem by lying on their backs in the water and holding the unopened shells on their chests. Then they smash the shells open with a rock. Egyptian vultures obviously heard about the otters' rock trick! (Or was it the other way around?) The vultures love ostrich eggs, but these eggshells are too hard to break with their beaks. So a vulture picks up a rock in its beak and throws it at the egg.

Other animals have also developed methods or tools to help them do things. Because termites don't like the sun, they make little paper umbrellas to use when they leave their mound. (Did termites or people make the first umbrella?) Of course, termites need to watch out for chimpanzees. Chimps love to eat termites! To help them find lots of these insects, chimpanzees make brushes by chewing the ends of sticks. Then they use the brushes to remove termites from a mound. And what does an elephant do when it has an itch on its back? What else? It picks up a stick with its trunk and scratches its back! Could it be, perhaps, that some animals are smarter than we think?

A. Exercising Your Skill

On a piece of paper, answer the following questions.

1. How would you state the main idea of this paragraph in your own words?
2. Does the sentence that best states the main idea of the passage come at the beginning, in the middle, or at the end? Copy that sentence on your paper.
3. What title would you give this passage?

B. Expanding Your Skill

Copy the following diagram on a piece of paper. Complete the main idea sentence in the center. On the adjoining lines, write some facts or details from the passage that support the main idea. Then add one of your own ideas. One has been done for you.

Most animals are _____ smart.

Termites make paper umbrellas.

C. Exploring Language

In one or more paragraphs, describe something very clever or smart that is done by your pet or a friend's pet, or you may write about something extraordinary you have read about that an animal did. For example, newspapers once reported the case of a heroic dog in California. In the middle of the night, the dog smelled smoke in the house. It immediately woke everyone up. Because of the dog, no one was hurt. On the other hand, you also may write about more ordinary behavior, but behavior that is still smart and clever. For example, your cat may be able to open a kitchen cabinet, get out a pouch of cat food, and rip it open, all by itself! Make sure that each paragraph you write has a main idea sentence.

D. Expressing Yourself

Choose one of these activities.

1. If your pet could talk for only fifteen minutes, what would you want it to talk about? Make a list of questions that you would ask your pet. Then make a second list of questions that your pet might want to ask you. Then, with a classmate, present a TV interview for the rest of the class. Play the role of your pet as your classmate plays "you" and asks your questions. Then play yourself and have your classmate ask your pet's questions.

2. With several classmates hold a debate on the following topic: *Which animals make better pets, dogs or cats?* Before you start the debate, write down all the reasons, or arguments, that support one side or the other. Make sure that you support your opinion with examples or facts. Hold the debate before the rest of the class. At the end of the debate, ask the audience to vote on which side had the stronger arguments.

3. Animals have been the heroes of many stories, both in real life and in fiction. They have saved people's lives by scaring away enemies, carrying messages, warning of danger, serving as guides, and so on. Make up a brief story in which an animal is the hero. Write it in the form of a newspaper report. Include a headline that states the main idea of the story and catches the reader's interest.

4. Go to the library and find information about one of these topics: (a) a group of very smart chimpanzees and gorillas that have learned to speak with sign language; (b) how marine biologists work with dolphins to study the way these animals communicate and how this research may prove to be useful someday. Ask the librarian to help you find articles about your topic in magazines or books. Take notes and then organize your notes for a report that you could give orally in class.

Everyone knows what a bank is. Even specialty "banks" such as blood banks are common today. However, have you ever heard of a "time bank"?

William Kaufman, a financial-planning consultant, knows that time is money. He created the concept of a time bank for employees who would *voluntarily* donate their unused paid time—vacation days, sick days, personal time, or overtime. The time, freely given by the employees, would be converted to dollars, or the cash value of the employees' time. The money would then be deposited in an interest-earning account in a commercial bank. This money would be given only to those company co-workers who needed extra time off from work at full pay.

Who would decide which were in need of such time? An employee–management committee would be set up at the participating company. A co-worker in need might be someone who was not covered by insurance for a personal crisis.

Many people think the time bank has come not a minute too soon!

---

1. The best title is—
   (A) Extra Time
   (B) A Financial-planning Consultant
   (C) Banking Time for Co-workers in Need
   (D) Losing Your Paid Vacation

2. The story says that William Kaufman created—
   (A) a free vacation   (B) a fitness program
   (C) a blood bank   (D) a time bank

3. Workers who donate time to the bank do so—
   (A) hastily   (B) freely
   (C) reluctantly   (D) unhappily

4. The story suggests that the idea of a time bank—
   (A) has come too soon   (B) may not be used by all employees
   (C) is not legal   (D) is better than a blood bank

5. The word "voluntarily" in line five means—
   (A) bravely   (B) surprisingly
   (C) willingly   (D) unwillingly

Americans celebrate their parents. There is Mother's Day on the second Sunday in May and Father's Day on the third Sunday in June. What about a holiday that honors the parents of parents? Michael Goldar took care of that. Naturally, he was a grandfather himself.

Goldar got the idea when he visited his elderly aunt. It upset him to see older people—once respected family members—no longer so valued. Goldar spent seven years, took seventeen trips to Washington, D.C., and spent $11,000 of his own money trying to gain acceptance for a holiday honoring grandparents. Finally, in 1978, Goldar's dream became a reality. President Jimmy Carter signed the *proclamation* making Grandparent's Day an annual national holiday on the Sunday after Labor Day.

What do Americans do for their grandparents on this special day? For one thing, they send grandparents more than four million greeting cards!

1. The best title is—
   (A) Three Special Sundays
   (B) Michael Goldar Is a Grandfather
   (C) A Grandfather Campaigns for Grandparent's Day
   (D) Grandparents Receive Millions of Cards

2. Goldar got the idea for Grandparent's Day when he visited—
   (A) President Carter   (B) his grandchildren
   (C) his aunt   (D) his grandparents

3. Grandparent's Day in America is celebrated on the—
   (A) Sunday after Labor Day   (B) third Sunday in June
   (C) Fourth of July   (D) second Sunday in May

4. The two national holidays that grandparents have in their honor are—
   (A) Grandparent's Day and   (B) Thanksgiving Day and Mother's
       Mother's or Father's Day   Day
   (C) Labor Day and Memorial Day (D) Grandparent's Day and their
                                      birthday

5. The word "proclamation" in line ten means—
   (A) public announcement   (B) greeting card
   (C) private treaty   (D) warning

The United Way is an organization that collects donations from people and companies. It uses the money to help finance many charities. When the Topeka Goodyear Tire Plant and its workers donated a record amount of money to the United Way, it used an unusual sign to advertise it—the world's largest tire.

Made at the Topeka plant, the tire weighed 12,000 pounds. It was called a Nylosteel tire because it was made of nylon and steel belts. Since it stood eleven feet high and nearly six feet wide, many people wondered—what could use such *monstrous* tires? The answer was a giant earthmover that can pick up enough dirt in one scoop to fill an average bedroom.

The people at the Topeka plant thought that the tire, with huge letters telling of their large contribution, was an excellent sign.

---

1. The best title is—
   (A) Helping Unfortunate People
   (B) Using the World's Largest Tire as a Sign
   (C) The Workers at the Topeka Tire Plant
   (D) The United Way

2. The world's largest tire is used on—
   (A) a truck   (B) an airplane
   (C) an earthmover   (D) a bus

3. The huge tire in the story is—
   (A) eleven feet high (B) four feet wide
   (C) made of plastic   (D) not expensive

4. You can conclude that the workers in the plant were proud of—
   (A) Topeka   (B) Goodyear
   (C) the 12,000 pound tire (D) the earthmover

5. The word "monstrous" in line eight means—
   (A) tiny   (B) common
   (C) huge   (D) new

UNIT 42

Puerto Rico still honors Captain Juan de Amezquita's heroism. In 1625, a Dutch fleet invaded the island. Captain Amezquita led a counterattack that temporarily halted the Dutch advance. The Dutch, however, continued forward and besieged the city of San Juan. According to legend, the Dutch general proposed a duel to the death to decide San Juan's fate. If the Dutch duelist won, San Juan would become a Dutch city.

The governor of Puerto Rico turned to Amezquita to defend the city. The duel took place on the walls of the impressive El Morro fortress. For hours Amezquita fenced with the Dutch champion. Finally, Juan's chest was pierced. As his *foe* raised his sword in victory, Amezquita, with his last breath, killed the Dutch general. Captain Juan de Amezquita then died victorious. The city of San Juan had been saved.

1. The best title is—
   (A) The Governor of Puerto Rico
   (B) Captain Amezquita Saves San Juan
   (C) San Juan—A Dutch City
   (D) El Morro Fortress

2. San Juan's fate was decided by a—
   (A) naval battle   (B) pistol
   (C) duel   (D) game

3. Amezquita and the Dutch champion fought with—
   (A) guns   (B) spears
   (C) bare fists   (D) swords

4. Captain Juan de Amezquita was probably born in—
   (A) Mexico   (B) Puerto Rico
   (C) the United States (D) Holland

5. The word "foe" in line ten means—
   (A) friend   (B) enemy
   (C) army   (D) follower

Clarence DeMar found out early that he could run better than he could walk. He was born in 1888 with *spinal* problems, which made him walk with a shuffle. At the age of eight, Clarence would run, not walk, from farmhouse to farmhouse near his home in Ohio selling sewing goods. At the age of eleven, he attended a trade school on an island in Boston Bay, Massachusetts. The boy would run all over the island to strengthen his legs.

Later, DeMar had to drop out of college to work as a printer. His place of work was seven miles from his house. Of course, DeMar ran back and forth to work. Running saved him the bus money, but, more important, running was something he loved to do.

In 1910, DeMar entered his first Boston Marathon. This famous race, which covers over twenty-six miles, then attracted two hundred runners from around the world. That year he finished second, but the following year he won. Over the years, DeMar "ran away with" a total of seven victories in the Boston Marathon.

1. The best title is—
   (A) The Boston Marathon
   (B) DeMar's Hard-earned Money
   (C) The Boy Who Loved to Run
   (D) A Pack of Runners

2. Clarence DeMar could run better than he could—
   (A) sew   (B) save money
   (C) sell door-to-door   (D) walk

3. The Boston Marathon covers—
   (A) over 7 miles   (B) 200 miles
   (C) over 26 miles   (D) 10 miles

4. All the running DeMar did in his younger years was good training for—
   (A) his old age   (B) the Boston Marathon
   (C) his farm work   (D) his work as a printer

5. The word "spinal" in line two means—
   (A) of the eyes   (B) being slow and stiff
   (C) of the backbone   (D) being too tall and thin

Few of the many stories about devoted dogs lead to a living memorial like the one in Montana called "The Shep Fund." The money collected goes to a school for deaf and blind children in Great Falls.

The dog Shep belonged to a sheepherder. He worked faithfully for years beside his master. When the man died, all Shep understood was that a black box was loaded onto a train. Shep watched the train pull away and settled down to wait for his master's return.

He spent the rest of his life at the station, meeting trains and looking for his master. The stationmaster fed him. During the dog's *vigil*, people tried to adopt him, but he was devoted to his master. When Shep finally died, one of the railroad conductors wrote his story, had it printed, and sold it to passengers. Thus began the "Shep Fund" that has been in existence for more than forty years.

---

1. The best title is—
   (A) A Sheepherder Dies
   (B) Trains in Montana
   (C) A Faithful Dog
   (D) A Kind Railroad Man

2. Money collected for "The Shep Fund" is given to a school for—
   (A) training dogs   (B) railroad workers
   (C) deaf and blind children   (D) newspaper writers

3. The story of Shep was written by a—
   (A) newspa   man   (B) sheepherder
   (C) train   ssenger   (D) railroad conductor

4. The story suggests that Shep was unusually—
   (A) dangerous   (B) foolish
   (C) loyal   (D) unfaithful

5. The word "vigil" in line nine means—
   (A) train ride   (B) years as a pup
   (C) period of watching and waiting   (D) period of happiness and joy

Pizza is one of America's favorite foods. No one is positive how it originated, although many people claim to know. Everyone agrees, however, that it was first made in Italy. Some Italians give credit to the city of Naples, and others give Sicily the honor.

Wherever the idea started, someone probably was baking bread, decided to put a little cheese and tomato sauce on top, and slipped it into the oven. Out came the world's first pizza.

Although pizza was thought of as a poor man's food in Italy, it was a king who first made pizza a popular food for everyone. In the seventeenth century, King Ferdinand of Bourbon was impressed by a certain cook's pizza. The King made him the royal *chef* and ordered him to make pizza often. The chef later wrote a cookbook in which he told how to make pizza, the King's delight.

1. The best title is—
   (A) Foods from Italy
   (B) How to Make Pizza
   (C) The Story of Pizza
   (D) A Royal Cookbook

2. Pizza was first made in—
   (A) Italy
   (B) France
   (C) Austria
   (D) the United States

3. The story says that the first pizza was probably made with—
   (A) sausage
   (B) spaghetti
   (C) cheese
   (D) peppers

4. Before pizza became a popular food, it was probably eaten most often by—
   (A) kings
   (B) Americans
   (C) bankers
   (D) common workers

5. The word "chef" in line eleven means—
   (A) king
   (B) artist
   (C) carpenter
   (D) cook

"Thanks" is always appreciated—even when it's a bit late. In 1926 Elvin Tarlow, then fourteen, had just passed his junior lifesaving test, and was patrolling the beach at Portland, Oregon, hoping he would have a chance to show off his new skill. Glimpsing a figure struggling in the surf, he dashed in and pulled seventeen-year-old Maybell McNutt to safety. Maybell recovered. Later she went on to study music and become a distinguished pianist and teacher of music at Lewis and Clark College. Fifty years passed, during which she did not see Elvin Tarlow again.

Then Maybell had a stroke and was confined to a rest home. In Maybell's notes, the home's social services director happened to see the name of Elvin Tarlow, who, by coincidence, was a friend of hers. Quickly the director arranged a reunion, and Maybell's sagging spirits were soon *buoyed* as she met her rescuer again—half a century later. She presented him with a framed letter of thanks, a little late but certainly deserved!

---

1. The best title is—
   (A) The Career of Maybell McNutt
   (B) A Thank-you After Fifty Years
   (C) A Family Reunion
   (D) A College Teacher Retires

2. When Elvin Tarlow saved Maybell, he was—
   (A) 17 years old   (B) 50 years old
   (C) 21 years old   (D) 14 years old

3. Maybell went to a rest home because she had a—
   (A) heart attack   (B) broken leg
   (C) stroke   (D) sprained ankle

4. The story suggests that Maybell had always meant to—
   (A) be a lifeguard   (B) study music
   (C) thank Elvin   (D) forget Elvin

5. The word "buoyed" in line twelve means—
   (A) raised   (B) ruined
   (C) doubted   (D) calmed

Can you imagine the Dust Bowl? No, it isn't a kitchen item or an old stadium where athletes compete. The Dust Bowl refers to those areas of the U.S. prairie states that have a great many dust storms.

In the 1930s, the Dust Bowl reached its greatest extent when the grasslands that had been plowed for wheat were abandoned because of poor farming practices. Much of the *topsoil* in states from North Dakota south to Texas lay unprotected. Raging winds then swept the dusty soil into the air. During these same years, a great economic depression forced thousands of farmers to leave their land to find work elsewhere. In Dust Bowl areas such as northwest Oklahoma and the eastern plains of Colorado, a severe drought worsened the soil erosion.

To understand what it was like living in the Dust Bowl at that time, imagine giant black clouds of dust rolling over your house. Dust and sand swirl in through windows and under doors and settle everywhere. That was the Dust Bowl.

---

1. The best title is—
   (A) Sandstorms
   (B) Soil Erosion
   (C) Great Years in the Prairie States
   (D) The Scene of the Dust Bowl

2. The Dust Bowl is—
   (A) a stadium   (B) a region
   (C) a kitchen item   (D) a state

3. The Dust Bowl was at its worst during—
   (A) the 1940s   (B) the night
   (C) the 1930s   (D) the day

4. The story suggests that the grasslands had once protected—
   (A) the cows   (B) the barns
   (C) the winds   (D) the soil

5. The word "topsoil" in line six means—
   (A) the heaviest soil   (B) soil beneath the ground
   (C) soil at the surface of the ground   (D) soil not good for growing crops

"He had furnished us with land and the four walls of a log cabin." Proud twelve-year-old Anna tells of her father's basic preparation for their family as they began a new life in the Michigan wilderness. In 1858, six members of the family, including Anna and her mother, went to live there on their own until Anna's father and two of the other children could join them. Anna goes on to describe the *isolation* of their new homestead. It was many miles from the nearest neighbor, railroad, or post office. In order to cook or bathe, the family had to carry water in pails from the creek.

Their first morning in the log cabin, they held a family council to discuss what had to be done first. It seemed that everything was needed urgently. The cabin had only holes where the doors and windows should be. There was no furniture or floor to speak of, just two chairs and the dirt beneath.

Amazingly, Anna went on to become a medical doctor. Years later, when Dr. Anna Howard Shaw was in her sixties, she recalled her pioneer days in her autobiography *The Story of a Pioneer*.

---

1. The best title is—
   (A) Anna's Life as a Young Pioneer
   (B) The Michigan Wilderness
   (C) Anna Becomes a Doctor
   (D) Dr. Anna Howard Shaw's Father

2. Anna did not write about her life in the wilderness until she was—
   (A) sixty   (B) two
   (C) five   (D) twelve

3. Anna says that the only objects in the cabin were—
   (A) two doors   (B) two chairs
   (C) two windows   (D) floorboards

4. You can tell that the story about Anna and her family—
   (A) never really happened   (B) happened recently
   (C) happened in the wintertime   (D) really happened

5. The word "isolation" in line six means—
   (A) joys   (B) confusion
   (C) loneliness   (D) comforts

Mozart, whom many consider the world's greatest composer, once accepted a challenge from his teacher, Franz Joseph Haydn. Haydn wagered that Mozart could not compose a piece of music that Haydn, an accomplished pianist, couldn't play. In five minutes, Mozart handed Haydn what looked like a simple little tune.

Haydn began to play. It seemed easy. Suddenly, he found that his left hand was playing at the extreme left of the keyboard and his right hand was at the far right. Then, amazingly, the music called for a note to be played right in the middle—at the same time.

The *irate* Haydn stopped playing and shouted that the bet was off. No one could play this music! Mozart calmly sat down and played. At the proper moment he bent over and struck the middle note—with his nose! Haydn paid the bet.

---

1. The best title is—
   (A) Music Long Ago
   (B) The Great Franz Haydn
   (C) Mozart Wins a Bet
   (D) A Dangerous Trick

2. The story says that Haydn was Mozart's—
   (A) cousin   (B) teacher
   (C) enemy   (D) friend

3. When Mozart played the tune, he used his—
   (A) toe   (B) elbow
   (C) nose   (D) ear

4. The story suggests that—
   (A) Mozart couldn't play the piano   (B) Haydn couldn't play the piano
   (C) Mozart had a sense of humor   (D) Mozart liked Haydn

5. The word "irate" in line ten means—
   (A) successful   (B) injured
   (C) angry   (D) brave

There are many unusual schools in America, and one of the most unusual is found in Oklahoma. In this school, the pupils learn how to shoe horses.

The school is Oklahoma Farrier's College in Sperry, Oklahoma. A "farrier" is a blacksmith. The course is eight weeks long. Students learn all about horses' legs and hooves, the different metals used for horseshoes, and how to heat and shape the metal into shoes. Then they learn how to apply the horseshoe to the hoof. They also study how to make *orthopedic* shoes to help horses with a limp or other walking problems.

Since the student blacksmiths need horses to practice on, the school offers farrier services to horse owners. Horse owners from miles around pay to have their horses fitted for new shoes. The service is so popular that sometimes the horses have to wait in a line a quarter of a mile long!

---

1. The best title is—
   (A) Shoeing a Horse
   (B) Learning About Horses
   (C) Free Horseshoes
   (D) A College for Blacksmiths

2. The school is located in—
   (A) Maine   (B) Delaware
   (C) Oklahoma   (D) Montana

3. The school offers—
   (A) free horses   (B) old shoes
   (C) farrier services   (D) horse training

4. The story suggests that the students—
   (A) come from big cities   (B) learn very little
   (C) get much practice   (D) dislike their work

5. The word "orthopedic" in line seven means—
   (A) women's   (B) designed to correct
   (C) designed to imitate   (D) dancing

In Unit 49, you read about Mozart. The early life of this composer is extremely interesting. Read this passage.

In 1756, a baby boy was born in Austria to Leopold Mozart and his wife. They named him Wolfgang Amadeus Mozart. It didn't take the parents long to realize that they had a most unusual son. At the age of three, Mozart was playing the harpsichord, a type of old-fashioned piano. And he had learned to play not from taking lessons but simply from watching and listening. At five he started to write music. His first piece almost wasn't played because some of the notes were hard to read—the little boy had made rather a mess with the ink! Before he turned six, however, he had written two short pieces called minuets for the harpsichord.

Leopold Mozart was a musician himself and played in a string quartet. One day the quartet was supposed to practice at his house. When the second violinist didn't show up, young Wolfgang was asked to take his place. He sat down, picked up the violin, and played the piece perfectly. His father and the other musicians couldn't believe their ears. Before that day the seven-year-old Mozart had never touched a violin. A year later, young Mozart wrote a complete symphony.

Tragically, Mozart died at the age of thirty-five. By then he had written about six hundred compositions ranging from operas to masses. Since his death, music lovers everywhere have always wondered what he would have created if only he had lived longer.

A. Exercising Your Skill

On a piece of paper, write the answers to these questions.

1. Which word or words would you use to describe Mozart's talent?
2. What clues in the passage helped you answer question 1?
3. What do you know about music and musicians today that also helped you answer question 1?

B. Expanding Your Skill

In the library find information about the early life of another composer, past or present. Choose one of the composers listed in the box below. As you read about the composer, take notes. Then organize in small groups according to composer studied. Compare with other groups how the composers are similar or different. At the end of the discussion, decide what important contributions to music each composer may have made.

Ludwig van Beethoven	Leonard Bernstein	Béla Bartók
John Philip Sousa	Scott Joplin	Richard Wagner

C. Exploring Language

Everyone has some special talent, even if it is not as great or obvious as Mozart's musical talent was. Think about a special talent that you have or that someone whom you admire very much has. It could be an obvious talent, such as an ability to draw, sing, or cook. Other talents are very important but not as easy to see or recognize. For example, you may understand computers and work easily with them. Other talents are related to personal qualities, such as generosity, leadership, or the ability to make people laugh.

Write a paragraph that describes what your own or someone else's special talent is, and give examples of how this talent is expressed. Explain when you first realized that this talent was special. Then tell how you (or the person you chose to write about) makes or could make use of this talent.

D. Expressing Yourself

Choose one of these activities.

1. Music changes over the years. The music Mozart wrote is very different from modern music, whether classical, jazz, or rock and roll. On your paper, make two columns. In the first column, list what you like about the music of today. In the second column, list what you dislike about it. Then compare your lists with your classmates' lists. Discuss this topic with your classmates: How does a person's taste in music reflect his or her personality?

2. Plan and put on a musical variety show. Urge classmates who sing or play musical instruments to participate. Some classmates can create an ad for the show. Others can write invitations to other classes or parents, and still others can make set decorations to be used for the performance.

3. You are the music critic for your school or local newspaper. Write a critical review of your favorite singer or musical group. Express your reaction to the singer's or group's latest release or performance. (Your review can focus on an actual record or concert.) Explain what you liked and what you did not like. Be sure to give examples to support your statements and opinions.

4. Create a musical collage. On a large piece of paper or cardboard, arrange pictures and symbols that express the theme "What music means to me." Exchange collages with a classmate and look over each other's pictures and symbols. Tell your classmate what you think music means to him or her, judging by the collage. Then have your classmate interpret your own collage.